CUBA REVISITED

My Story

Herman Martin

Pen Press Publishers Ltd

First published in Great Britain by
Pen Press Publishers Ltd
39, Chesham Road
Brighton
BN2 1NB

ISBN 1-905621-19-1
978-1-905621-19-4

Printed and bound in the UK

A catalogue record of this book is available from
the British Library

Cover design by Jacqueline Abromeit

Dedication

This book is dedicated to my friend Serena Saunders,
my sisters Carmen Hurgos and Pauline Irving,
cousins Michelle and Stephanie Poorman
and my special friend Andrea Almonte in the Dominican
Republic.

About the author

Herman Martin was born in Jamaica and came England in 1961. His passion for traveling and meeting people of different nationalities gave him the motivation to visit many countries including America, Canada, Eastern Europe, Latin America and the West Indies.

He is fascinated by history and has studied the subject in great depth. His inspiration and motivation to write have resulted in many of his articles being published in the local newspapers.

Acknowledgements

My gratitude and appreciation goes out to the following staff at Beaches Hotel, Varadero, for making my first visit to Cuba such an enjoyable and unforgettable one:

Emily: For taking the time off work to show me around Varadero. For inviting me to her home to meet her family and share their meals. Without Emily's inspiration and encouragement during my research, it would not be possible for me to gather all the information that I required.

Nancy: For devoting so much of her time giving me invaluable facts regarding the history of Cuba. For all the information regarding the historical and cultural places to visit, and for her role as my interpreter.

Miriela: For giving me such a warm welcome and ensuring that my visit to Cuba was an enjoyable one.

Pilar, Tamara, and the staff: For their kindness and devotion.

Odalys: For her kind invitation to meet her parents and her children, and for their overwhelming hospitality. For taking the time to show me around Santa Martha.

Tomás: For inviting me to meet his family, showing me around Cardenas, and for their generosity.

Laura, Emma, Iris and Marcoti: For their devotion and generosity.

My gratitude and appreciation also goes out to:

Sandra for her invaluable assistance, expertise and guidance in the compilation of this book.

Contents

Chapter		Page

CUBA REVISITED

My Story

Part 1

Introduction

As a young boy growing up in Jamaica, I could vividly recall hearing news about the revolution that was taking place in Cuba in 1957-1958. At such a young age, I had no idea what was meant by a revolution. At that time, there was no news media as such, and since my family never discussed politics, although Cuba is only ninety miles away, the outside world meant nothing to me.

However, I could recall an elderly distant cousin of mine, with both legs amputated, returning to Jamaica in 1960. I was informed that he had been living in Cuba for a number of years and had lost his legs due to the revolution. As far as everyone was concerned, that was the end of the story.

I then immigrated to England where I picked up bits and pieces of news relating to the American confrontation with the Russians over the Cuban missiles, the American aggressive embargo on Cuba, and their invasion at the Bay of Pigs in April 1961.

Over the next decade, my fascination towards Cuba gradually evolved to such an extent that I decided to get more in-depth knowledge of the history of the island and its people. Little did I know at the time that what was being broadcast by the imperialist American media was all propaganda to discredit the Cuban population, the revolution and its purpose.

As my fascination grew, I decided that I needed some realistic literature to satisfy my curiosity about the facts and myths about Cuba and its people. I was fortunate to acquire some material about the island, which was very rare to obtain any literature on Cuba. After studying the limited amount of material at my disposal, my urge was to visit Cuba, not as an everyday tourist as such, but rather a tourist on a "fact finding" visit.

I needed to do some exploring of the island, to meet the Cuban people, see their way of life, and to establish what were the facts and what were the myths. In 2001, I finally decided that the time had arrived for me to visit Cuba.

Unaware of what to expect, I decided that a stay of three weeks should be ample time to satisfy my curiosities. I opted for a seven day "Discover Cuba Tour" and fourteen days at the all-inclusive Beaches Hotel at Varadero. My tour took me to Havana, Cienfuegos, Sancti Spiritus, Santa Clara, and the beautiful town of Trinidad.

Chapter One

London Gatwick Airport

Wednesday, 30ᵗʰ May 2001

I was in the North Terminal of London Gatwick airport checking in for a flight that would change my life in a tremendous way. My destination was the island of Cuba in the West Indies, the country that I'd been dreaming of visiting for the past two decades. This was my day one, which filled me with great joy and emotion.

A problem free check-in allowed me over three hours to spare before boarding the Boeing 777 British Airways flight BA4505. Although still filled with emotions, I was able to have a snack and have a look around the airport. It seemed that I had been in a dream and hadn't woken up until I was on board the aircraft. My window seat was ideal which enabled me to see us taxiing down the runway. At this moment in time, I felt peace, joy and happiness. The cabin crew was exceptionally pleasant and helpful which made the flight quite enjoyable.

After nearly ten hours, I finally arrived in Cuba. Approaching Havana airport, in the mid-afternoon tropical sunshine, I could see the rolling hills, houses and traffic below. Although in a conscious state of mind, I found it hard to believe that I was in Cuba, that my dream had finally become reality.

Chapter 2

Havana Airport

Immigration and Customs

I was rather surprised how antiquated Havana airport seemed, now that Cuba had become renowned as a popular tourist destination. Not knowing what to expect, I was a little apprehensive regarding the immigration and customs procedures. However, with my travel documents (passport, tourist card and luggage receipt), I made my way to the immigration desk. Sitting in a cubicle was a stern looking immigration officer to whom I handed the documents. Very slowly and thoroughly he processed the documents, then passed them back to me. I then made my way to the baggage reclaim area to retrieve my luggage. With nothing to declare, I went through the "green" barrier to the reception area where the tour guide (Carlos), the mini bus driver, and the rest of the party were waiting.

I entered the bus and chose a seat by the window in order to get a good view of Cuba, the people, the rain soaked roads and the lush vegetation. I was still wondering if I was really in the country that I so much wanted to visit for the past two decades.

We introduced ourselves to one another: Peter and his wife Menna from Luton, and Ian from Inverness. Missing from the party was a couple from London whom I met at the hotel later in the evening. We set off in the tropical rainstorm for the forty-five minute drive to the Comodoro Hotel in new Havana where we stayed for three nights.

Chapter 3

The Comodoro Hotel

A large hotel set in beautiful tropical gardens with smartly built cottages surrounded by palm trees in the grounds. At the reception desk, I was overwhelmed by the warm and friendly attitude of the staff and how beautiful the girls were with such charming smiles on their faces. Dressed in crisply ironed blue uniforms, with skirts at least six inches above the knees, they were some of the most attractive girls I have ever seen.

At the check-in desk, I was allocated a very spacious and comfortable room on the third floor. From the balcony, the view overlooked the Atlantic Ocean dotted with fishing boats. The vast expanse of blue clear water and the setting sun over the horizon was the most spectacular scenery that I've ever seen.

I had arranged to meet Menna, Peter and Ian in the bar after a shower and a change of clothes. I arrived in the bar at 7.00 p.m. and was pleasantly surprised that there were so many varieties of drinks available.

The Restaurant

After a few drinks, we decided that we should go to dinner. With a choice of three restaurants, we were undecided which one to choose. After some deliberation, we opted for the à la carte.

The choices and quality of the menu were beyond my imagination, considering that there is an acute shortage of many products. Everything was plentiful and prepared to perfection. Nothing was left to be desired.

One couldn't help noticing how attractive and elegantly dressed the waitresses were in their uniforms.

Chapter 4

Discover Cuba - Day 1

Thursday, 31ˢᵗ May 2001

We met in the lobby of the Comodoro Hotel at 8.30 a.m. to discuss the itinerary for the first of a two-day tour of Havana. The group consisted of Carlos (the tour guide), Menna, Peter, Ian, the couple from London and myself.

Havana

Havana is a city whose reality surpasses its imagination and reputation. Havana is like nowhere on earth. The old and new Havana entwined itself with old, dilapidated colonial and beautiful sprawling buildings and fine, huge mansions surrounded with leafy parks.

It is a city of romantic grandeur, vibrancy and power with an added bonus of sheer beauty. Here you'll find hundreds of huge 1950s American cars cruising the streets, and stunning looking, elegantly dressed girls. It can be said that Cuban girls ooze natural beauty like a second layer of skin.

My trip took me around new Havana which boasts huge modern hotels nestled among palm trees and tropical gardens of sheer grandeur.

The Miramar district of Fifth Avenue (Avenida 5) boasts smart pink painted villas and embassies surrounded by neatly kept lawns and leafy parks. The drive along the 5 kilometre (3 mile) length of the Malecón was an experience I shall never forget. The Malecón

(Habanero) so called by the Cubans, is more than a long wall by the coast. It is a living witness of so many generations that throughout the centuries have spent warm and relaxed evenings there. Every day one can notice students, friends, couples, people of all ages walking by or just sitting there on the wall dating or just enjoying the refreshing tropical breeze. The tropical heat engulfed by the cool sea's breeze is an experience of sheer delight and fascination. Some of the most magnificent buildings including the Riviera and Nacional hotels can be found along the Malecón.

This is Havana, which gives an aura of vibrancy, power and sheer beauty which makes it so special. I found the contrast between the new and old Havana astounding.

The new parts of the city can be described as very up market with magnificent houses, embassies and hotels, while the old part consists of hundreds of colonial dilapidated buildings. Yet it possesses charm, culture and character. A massive restoration project has been taking place for many years costing millions of dollars.

Among the charms of old Havana are the grand cathedrals, museums and galleries consisting of thousands of priceless antiques and paintings. During my visits to La Real Fuerza Fortress (Cuba's oldest military structure), Cathedral Square, Havana Cathedral, Prado Promenade, Capitol Building, and the craft markets with fine carvings, beautifully handmade garments, and superb paintings by local artists, I realised why Cuba is unlike any other place on earth.

Chapter 5

Discover Cuba - Day 2

Friday, 1st June 2001

After breakfast, we met in the hotel lobby at 9.00 a.m. to discuss the itinerary for the second and final day tour of Havana. We decided to do another mini tour of new Havana before moving on to the old part of the city.

I was fascinated by the beauty of this part of the capital with its huge modern buildings, splendid landscaped gardens, and well-kept extra wide roads.

My visit to Plaza de la Revolución (Revolution Square) was the most magical moment I'd ever experienced. Here I felt at home, a sense of power and tranquillity, a sense of belonging. I was fascinated by the huge portrait of Che Guevara, which adorns the front of one of the many huge government buildings that surrounds the square. In amazement, I stood alone and reflected on the people's response to Fidel Castro's historical speech to his victorious comrades of the revolution; the longest speech that has ever been made, which lasted more than seven hours on 8th January 1959. I could hear the cheers; feel the power, the harmony of the people as if I were present on such a memorable occasion.

My tour continued to Finca La Vigia, the home of the late Ernest Hemingway. The house still contains his personal possessions, which includes his hunting trophies, typewriter, books, chairs and desk. Due to strict preservation control, visitors are not allowed inside, but photographs can be taken using non-flash cameras.

My tour of Havana ended with a visit to Hemingway's famous bars: El Floridita and La Bodequita del Medio.

Havana can be described as a city which comprises mystery, aura, magic, history, sadness and laughter. Similar to most cities, there are street hustlers selling almost anything from rum to cigars that are generally of inferior quality.

On display are weapons captured from the invading Americans during the Bay of Pigs confrontation.

Here you'll find the very overcrowded camel buses where the limit on the number of passengers is nonexistent.

Havana, with its huge 1950s cars, galleries, museums, cathedrals, universities, famous bars and restaurants oozes charm and culture that's incomparable.

Chapter 6

Cienfuegos

Saturday, 2nd June 2001

I met the other members of the party at 9.00 a.m. in the lobby of the Comodoro hotel.

After spending two sensational and unforgettable days in Havana, today was to be the start of a further four days tour exploring some of the most magnificent historic and cultural sites and towns in Cuba.

We left the hotel at 10.00 a.m. for the first destination, the city of Cienfuegos – the third largest city in Cuba.

I was surprised how well maintained the highways were, except for the very few rough patches. In common with Cuba's highways, flowers and palm trees are planted along the central reservations, which enhanced the beauty of the countryside. I was overwhelmed at the lush green vegetation, the thousands of acres of sugar cane and citrus fruit plantations.

Cienfuegos, situated at the curve of a great bay, makes it broad and airy, with the Paseo del Pradó running right through the centre onto the Malecón (seafront) lined with huge colonial houses. It is a city full of life with its pedestrian thoroughfare (the Avenida San Fernando), the haunt of the most beautiful girls, many of French origin. It can be said that the women of Cienfuegos are the most elegant in Cuba.

My visit to the Galeria de Arte Universal and the Museo Historico, with its collection of fine antique furniture, revealed the cultural achievements of Cienfuegos.

The city boasts perfectly planned, exceptionally wide streets, harmoniously combined with outstanding buildings and other architectural beauties, giving an aura and splendour of a cosmopolitan culture with a strong French accent. This is a city that should, and will be, one of the top tourist attractions of Cuba for many future years.

After spending a night at the Faro Luna Hotel, I looked forward to my trip to Trinidad and Sancti Spiritus.

Chapter 7

Trinidad

Sunday, 3rd June 2001

We met in the lobby of the Faro Luna Hotel at 9.00 a.m. after breakfast to discuss the trip for the day which took us to the town of Trinidad.

The journey along the highway was one of fascination and enjoyment. The rolling hills, rugged mountains and the lush vegetation displayed scenery of sheer beauty.

Trinidad, listed as the most beautiful town in Cuba, is the best-preserved and most intact with its cobble-stoned streets steeped in tradition and legend.

The beautifully preserved colonial town centre is full of elegant villas in pastel shades of blue and yellow. I was overwhelmed by the beautiful mansions, public buildings, religious structures and wooden balustrades. Trinidad, with its tiled roofs, magnificent wrought-iron window grilles and wooden mansions can be regarded as a museum town, the home of the finest arts in Cuba.

The town specialises in traditional outstanding needlework, ceramics, embroidery, latticework and beautiful handmade decorations.

Listed as a world heritage site by UNESO in 1989, it lies on the Caribbean coast and the unique refreshing tropical sea breeze gives it a special atmosphere.

Similar to all Cuban towns, the central square, Plaza Mayor, is the focus of attention for siestas, music and gorgeous girls; a superbly laid out square, shaded by palm trees and surrounded by huge private houses, hotels and restaurants.

My tour of Trinidad took me up a narrow winding stairway to the tower of the Museo de Arqueologia Guamuhaya, from where the view stretches over the entire town.

With a population of 50,000, Trinidad was a peaceful, sleepy town maintaining a slow pace of horse-drawn carriages over its narrow cobble-stoned streets until 1991 when the first tourists arrived. Since then, the town has become a top tourist destination generating well-needed revenue into the economy.

Chapter 8

Sancti Spiritus

Monday, 4th June 2001

Today, my sixth day in Cuba, and so far this had been a holiday of a lifetime, full of excitement and astonishment.

After breakfast at the Rancho Hatuey in Trinidad, I set off on my journey to Sancti Spiritus, which continued to the immortal and historic town of Santa Clara. The journey along the highway was one of charm and inspiration; the cattle, horses and goats grazing freely with no care in the world, was a scene I hadn't seen for over four decades. In common with Cuba's agricultural sectors, there are thousands of acres of sugar cane and citrus fruit plantations.

Sancti Spiritus is a truly colonial, sleepy, town situated in the heart of the island with very few tourists, yet charming with a typical Cuban setting and atmosphere.

Chapter 9

Santa Clara

Santa Clara, situated in the agricultural heartland of Cuba, is a town of immortality.

Santa Clara is undoubtedly a living memory to Che Guevara and his comrades' victory over the dictator Batista. The town immortalized Che as the hero of the revolution after his victory of the famous battle of December 1958. It was here that Che received news that an armoured ammunitions train was about to pass near the town, going south. With only a few men and a bulldozer, he managed to capture the impregnable wagons. This gave the revolutionaries ample weapons to turn the tide of the war.

On 1st January 1959, Fidel Castro made a victorious entry into Havana, followed by Che and Camilo Cienfuegos on 18th January.

Santa Clara is proud of its victorious past. So much so that the famous hotel had been renamed Santa Clara Libre (free Santa Clara). Although it has been repainted green, they have kept the bullet holes in the front of the building. The hotel overlooks the Parque Vidal, which lies in the heart of the town. In common with all town centre parks in Cuba, here you will find lots of activities. During recreation time at the nearby secondary school, the park is filled with schoolgirls smartly dressed in their uniforms of white blouses and yellow skirts.

As I stood silently in the square opposite the Santa Clara Libre Hotel, I could visualise the tactics and movements of the comrades, the bombardment of the town, and the final victory of the combatants.

To the west of Santa Clara, the most famous monument is the Mausoleum of Che Guevara, which contains the remains of the great leader and his comrades since October 1997. The remains were discovered in Bolivia thirty years after they were assassinated. As I entered the mausoleum, I was immediately overcome with joy and sadness, yet felt so proud and humble to be there, a place of sober contemplation. It had been a moment in time that was unforgettable.

I stood in the square, Plaza de la Revolución Che Guevara, deep in thought, admiring the dominating seven metre bronze statue of Che which was erected in 1987 to mark the twentieth anniversary of the great revolutionary leader's death. Inscribed on the base of the statue, in fitting tribute are the words "hasta la victoria siempre" – ever onwards to victory.

For the first time in my life this was the place where I felt joy, peace, tranquillity and a sense of belonging.

Tuesday, 5th June 2001
Santa Clara to Beaches Hotel – Varadero

After breakfast at the Granjita hotel, I set off on the two-hour trip to Beaches Hotel, Varadero – my residence for the next fifteen nights. It had been a beautiful morning – clear blue sky, brilliant sunshine, with the usual Caribbean Sea breeze.

The journey took me along some of the most spectacular scenery that I have ever seen. Thousands of acres of citrus fruit and sugar cane, green lush vegetation, animals grazing freely in the fields, and the mountains risen high in the background. With people selling fruit and vegetables by the side of road, some hitchhiking to their destinations, others going about their business at such leisurely paces, it seemed that the world had ground to a halt.

After one of the most enjoyable journeys, I arrived at the beautiful town of Varadero, basking in the mid-afternoon tropical sunshine with the palm trees swaying to and fro from the tropical sea breeze.

Chapter 10

The Beaches Hotel – Varadero

After seven days touring and six hotels, I was looking forward to my fourteen days at Beaches Hotel. A truly magnificent hotel set in twenty acres of rich tropical grounds on the stunning Varadero beach. The main building consists of 350 junior suites plus a number of cottages scattered around the grounds. I was quite pleased that I had chosen one of the concierge suites situated on the fourth floor overlooking the beautiful gardens, swimming pools and the sea in the distance.

The hotel provides a varied number of activities to cater for everyone's needs, including Latin American dance lessons, cabaret, fashion show, tennis, disco and theme nights. As an all-inclusive hotel, the choice of menu and the quality of the meals were outstanding. I was particularly surprised that so many top brands of drinks were available in the bars and in the hotel suite. With four restaurants and four bars on site, the choices were limitless.

The Beach

A truly magnificent beach of pure white sand stretching for miles. Very large and clean with beach huts scattered around, providing ample space for all the guests.

Chapter 11

The Staff

Emily: One of the three staff in charge of the concierge suites greeted me (the others were Nancy and Miriela, to whom I shall give further mention). Emily was the most attractive girl that I've ever seen. Dark skinned, teeth as white as snow, dressed in uniform of white blouse and red mini skirt at least six inches above the knees. She spoke perfect English, was very intelligent, walked elegantly with such femininity she oozed beauty and charm. Emily possessed such flair and sophistication, yet so humble and gracious.

Nancy: As one of the three staff in charge of the concierge suites, I was always in contact with Nancy, a very attractive and charming girl, very intelligent and inspiring. In a later chapter, I shall comment on the overwhelming support that Nancy gave me in my quest to write this book.

Miriela: The third member of staff in charge of the concierge suites. An attractive and stunning girl whose presence was always felt whenever she entered the room, a girl full of charm and sophistication.

The Staff: All were smartly dressed in well-ironed uniforms, always smiling with the warmest of welcome for all the guests.

I was very impressed by their professionalism and mannerism. Each member of staff had been well organised, considerate and displayed an abundance of etiquette. They strive in giving full satisfaction and, like all Cubans, are very appreciative.

Chapter 12

Emily's Family

During my first four days at Beaches Hotel, Emily and I got on so well with each other it appeared as if we were old acquaintances.

Since one of my main objectives for visiting Cuba was to get some insight of the everyday lifestyle of the ordinary Cubans, I was delighted when Emily invited me to her home to meet her family. Unknown to me at the time, this turned out to be the first of three visits. I shall describe my other visits in a later chapter.

On my arrival I was greeted by Emily's parents, who unfortunately didn't speak a word of English. However, they were very welcoming and I immediately felt at home, as if I were part of the family. The next arrival was Emily's brother who lived just outside Santa Martha and, although he didn't speak English (Emily being the interpreter), we got along very well. The rest of the family, Emily's daughter, her sister and brother-in-law, I met on one of my other visits.

During my first twelve days in Cuba, I had discovered that many basic everyday items such as stationery, toiletries, and food products were in very short supply.

I was very grateful (if somewhat surprised) that I was asked to join the family for refreshments, which included typical home grown Cuban coffee, which was served very strong with no milk. For the first (and not the last) time, I had discovered the kind disposition of the Cuban people.

The Family Home

Although a moderate size house, I was quite impressed by the furnishings. Everything was neatly arranged, and in common with all Cuban homes, the electric fan and rocking chair took centre stage. With a fine display of photographs, ornaments, carvings and paintings, I felt a sense of pride that the Cubans possess.

From my observation, it was quite obvious that the Cubans are a close-knit family.

Chapter 13

Day Trips from The Beaches Hotel, Varadero

Since one of my main objectives for visiting Cuba was to discover as many places as possible during my three-week stay, I decided to take full advantage of the organised day trips.

This was an added bonus as it gave me the chance to meet the ordinary Cubans, and other tourists from various countries such as Canada, Africa, Europe and Latin America.

My trips took me on a boat ride on a man-made canal to Guama, a replica Taino Indian village, a nature reserve and crocodile farm. I also took a catamaran cruise on the Atlantic Ocean and a mini submarine trip to see some of the most amazing corals, and a shoal of over twenty-five different species of fish.

It was an overwhelming experience to have visited Playa Girón (Bay of Pigs); the site of the 1963 invasion of the CIA backed Americans who were defeated within seventy-two hours of landing on Cuban soil.

CUBA REVISITED

My Story

Part 2

Introduction

My first trip to Cuba in May/June 2001 was such an inspiring and fascinating experience that my decision for another visit in July 2002 was taken without hesitation.

Once again, my choice of hotel was Beaches Varadero, mainly due to its location, facilities, restaurants, bars and exceptionally friendly staff.

My two-week stay could be seen as a working holiday, since I needed to discover a great deal more about the island, its people, heritage and historical sites.

The duration of my stay enabled me to visit towns such as Residential Varadero, Havana, Camaguey, Santa Martha and Cárdenas.

Chapter 14

London Heathrow/Havana Airports

Monday, 8th July, 2002

I arrived at London Heathrow Airport at 10.00 a.m. for Air Jamaica flight JM004 en route on my second visit to Cuba.

I checked in four hours ahead of the scheduled flight time, which allowed me ample time to have breakfast and look around the terminal. Having completed all the formalities and a visit to the duty free shop, it was now time for the boarding procedures.

After a delay of almost two hours, we eventually took off at 4.00 pm. The all female Jamaican cabin crew were some of the most beautiful girls that I've ever seen, and with the in-flight fashion show and aerobics, the flight was most enjoyable.

After a ten-hour flight and quite a bit of air turbulence, I was once again in Cuba. On the approach to touch down, the green fields, buildings and traffic below brought back some emotional memories. Similar to my first visit 12 months previously, I was overcome with joy, peace and tranquillity.

I completed the immigration and customs procedures in a relatively short time, and with the help of a cigar-smoking porter, I collected my luggage and was met by the Kuoni representative for the two-and-a-half hour drive to Beaches Hotel, Varadero. Due to the darkness and pouring rain, there wasn't much to see, but I looked forward to the next two weeks of sheer bliss and enjoyment.

I eventually arrived at the hotel at 12.30 a.m. where I met Nancy at the reception desk. She had been transferred, on request, from the concierge office to reception duties. She was very pleased to have seen me and expressed her appreciation on my return to Beaches hotel. We talked about the events of the past 12 months, the staff changes, Mirela and Emily.

Tuesday, 9th July 2002

Although jetlagged and a very late night, I decided to take an early morning stroll around the hotel complex to see what changes had been made since my last visit.

The only visible changes were the cabaret area and pool bar, which had been modernised to give a friendlier atmosphere.

At 8.30 a.m. I decided to have breakfast in the main restaurant. I was immediately recognised by Ivette, one of the waitresses. With her usual charm, beauty and elegance, she gave me an exceptionally warm welcome.

Most of the day was spent on the beach and meeting many of the staff whom I'd met on my last visit. I was overwhelmed by the warm and passionate reception that I received from everyone.

Chapter 15

Hemingway Marina

Wednesday, 10th July 2002

My morning began with the normal routine: up at 6 a.m., showered, took a stroll on the beach, and then went for breakfast in the Reflections restaurant. In common with most Cuban restaurants, there was a good choice of food ranging from eggs, bacon, fresh fruits, cereals and fruit juices.

An invitation by some Canadian friends to visit Hemingway Marina was readily accepted. Named after the late Ernest Hemingway, it is constructed in an inlet of the Atlantic Ocean, just outside Havana. The modern marina moored many large and expensive boats and yachts, and the complex consisted of some beautiful buildings including a large restaurant surrounded by palm trees and well designed landscaped gardens.

On my return to the hotel, I was met by Emily and made arrangements to meet her family and take her out to lunch the following day.

Chapter 16

Varadero

Thursday, 11ᵗʰ July 2002

Varadero, situated on the North Coast, is Cuba's premier beach resort. Over the past decade the town has developed so rapidly that it now has its own international airport. It is a town of charm and beauty with sprawling hotels set in acres of beautifully manicured lawns, landscaped gardens displaying exotic tropical plants and flowers. Hotels such as Meliá Varadero, Club Méditerranee, Sandals Royal Hicacos Report & Spa, Brisas del Caribe and Beaches Varadero are rated among the best in the Caribbean and Latin America.

With the all-inclusive facilities and beautiful beaches, many tourists felt the need to remain in the resorts, but I needed to discover the true residential areas of Varadero. Moreover, one of my main objectives to visiting the island was to learn about Cuba and its people from an internal point of view.

This was made possible when I visited Emily's home to meet her parents as I did during my first trip. Not only did I meet her parents, but also her daughter, brother, sister and her husband.

I was delighted by the overwhelming reception that I received and immediately became aware that my visit was tremendously appreciated. Any misgivings that I had were soon to disappear when I discovered how loving, devoted and what a close-knit family they were, in common with all Cubans.

My jaunt around the town was one of sheer fascination. Mingled together are old colonial buildings, modern sprawling mansions, villas, hotels and restaurants.

I was totally surprised to see how well-stocked the shops were, selling everything from tee-shirts, paintings and carvings to picture postcards, the majority aimed at the tourist market. However, the lack of many everyday household products was obvious, due to the island's economic situation.

Emily and I had an enjoyable lunch at one of the many restaurants, which provided top of the range menus with an excellent service. I opted for the traditional dish of rice and black beans (a variety of kidney beans), roast chicken and vegetables. Dessert consisted of ice cream and fruit, finished off with Cuban coffee. Traditional meats such as chicken, pork and beef are the Cubans' favourite, and they are generally marinated and left overnight. This brings out the flavour, which is quite tasty and spicy. It is said that if the main meal does not contain meat, the Cuban insists that it is incomplete.

Chapter 17

Havana

Friday, 12th July 2003

My two-day tour of Havana in 2001 was such a fascinating experience that today I decided to pay another visit to one of the most exceptional, astonishing and breathtaking cities in the world. It is a city that exudes an air of grandeur, vibrancy and character.

The two and a half hour journey from Varadero on an ideal tropical morning (hot, sunny, clear blue sky, exhilarating sea breeze) was most enjoyable. The well maintained highways with flowers and palm trees along the central reservations, the green lush vegetation, thousands of acres of sugar cane and citrus fruits, the quaint villages and people strolling casually about as if the world had come to a halt, were beyond my imagination.

My tour of Havana took me to the famous Revolution Square renowned for Fidel Castro's record breaking non-stop seven-and-a-half hour speech, the Pope's massive audience, the huge illuminated face of Che Guevara and the monument erected to national hero José Marti.

My drive along the Malecón (the elegant five kilometre ocean drive that curves around the bay of Havana) was one of partial disappointment, since it was severely damaged by the hurricane in the latter part of 2001.

The up-market areas of Fifth Avenue (Avenida 5) and the residential Miramar district with its pink villas, sprawling mansions and embassies still displayed sheer charm and beauty. Visiting a cigar factory was an intriguing experience to see the tobacco leaves individually hand selected for the various brands of cigars, which are all individually hand made.

The highlight of the day was my visit to La Habana Vieja (old Havana), which boasts some of the most magnificent colonial buildings in Cuba. The Palicio de los Capitanes Generales, said to be the grandest palace in old Havana is situated in the city's oldest square, the Plaza de Armas. It is an exceptional building with unique arches, columns and a large marble staircase. It now houses the Museum of the City of Havana with its priceless collection of antiques, sculptures and paintings. One of the most unique features associated with the building is that the pavement outside is made of timber rather than concrete. This was done to reduce noises from footsteps disturbing the colonial occupiers.

Parque Central is one of the most popular and famous areas in Havana. Situated in the old part of the capital, there is fine architecture and huge 19th century hotels.

The Capitol building (Capitolio Nacional), built between 1929 and 1932 in a similar shape to the one in Washington with its 200ft white dome, is a featured landmark. It now houses the National Library of Science and Technology and the Cuban Academy of Sciences. Entry to this magnificent building is gained by a number of steps to the exceptionally large statue of Jupiter, which represents the state.

Nearby is the Partaga´s tobacco factory, one of the most famous and oldest factories in Cuba.

Havana can be said to be the best-preserved Spanish colonial city in the world. It has some of the world top entertainment venues including the Tropicana club, famous for its music and dance shows.

Chapter 18

Plaza America

Saturday, 13th July 2002

My visit took me to Plaza America, a smart shopping precinct situated next to the beautiful white sandy beach of Varadero. The Plaza comprises a number of modern up-market shops and boutiques.

The large well-stocked supermarket sells everything from groceries to household products, beers, wines and spirits.

All the ladies and gentlemen's outlets stocked very fashionable expensive items, which are specifically for the tourist market. This is reflected in the island's economy since the Government controlled wages is approximately US$10 per month.

The most renowned landmark is the Plaza America Convention Centre, a large modern building with a variety of facilities catering for tourism conventions.

Chapter 19

Camaguey

Sunday, 14th July, 2002

Camaguey is an exceptionally fine and glamorous city with a southern sensational atmosphere. It is a city with an intriguing road network system, where the twisting streets are laid out in every direction creating a maze of cul-de-sacs, narrow thoroughfares and one-way systems.

Many of the streets are a clutter of old tramlines with bicitaxis (rickshaws) racing each other at full speed with the blaring of bells and horns.

The city is famous for its popular ballet company, numerous cultural events, art and pottery exhibitions and extra wide terracotta pots, some of which can be thirteen feet in circumference.

Camaguey's main thoroughfare, Calle Republica, is closed to all traffic every Saturday evening, where the locals set up snack bars, eat, drink and dance in the middle of the street.

It is a prosperous city with huge sugar cane plantations and Cuba's largest dairy herds.

The Parque Agramonte, one of the prettiest plazas in Camaguey, is the main location where people arrange to meet each other.

The city has a number of famous and historic buildings such as Casa de la Trova (Ballad House) where the best musicians perform and the house of Nicolás Guillen, said to be the most famous poet during the revolution.

Chapter 20

.

Socialising

Monday, 15th – Thursday, 18th July 2002

Over the period of four days, I met some very nice guests from various countries such as Canada, England, Nigeria and South America. It was a pleasant and unexpected surprise when Emily introduced me to the hotel manager and his wife, a charming couple originally from Puerto Rico.

I was quite pleased to have met Odalys' (a member of staff) parents who kindly gave me an invitation to visit their home at Santa Martha on Friday 19th.

Having decided to take full advantage of the hotel facilities, we spent most of the days on the beach, at the pool, a visit to the dolphin aquarium and a catamaran cruise on the Atlantic Ocean. Most of the evenings and nights were spent in the bars, at the theme nights, which included cabaret, disco and fashion show. A night out at the Mambo Club was arranged for a fee of US$10, which included all the drinks that one could consume and the Latin American music. It turned out to be great fun.

Chapter 21

Santa Martha

Friday, 19th July 2002

Friday, 19th July 2002

A district situated a few miles from the tourist resort of Varadero, Santa Martha can be described as the typical Cuban residential area. Nestled among the ram-shackled houses are some smart modern buildings. There are scores of shabby looking high rise apartments with washing dangling from the balconies in the tropical sun. The sound of Latin American music could be heard blaring on every street. Although many basic items are in short supply, the shops are fairly well stocked, selling anything from clothes to electrical goods.

In the centre of the district is Odalys' apartment, which is situated on the third floor. From the outside the building looked in need of a facelift, but once inside I was pleasantly surprised on the smartness of the apartment. It was well decorated with modern furniture, top of the range hi-fi system, television and, as always, the rocking chair and electric fan took centre stage. The apartment is occupied by Odalys, her two children and her parents – an example of the Cuban's culture of the extended family.

As her parents' only language is Spanish, Odalys acted as my interpreter. I was invited to stay for lunch, which was traditionally Cuban – rice, black beans, vegetables and coffee. It was a very enjoyable meal, well prepared, very tasty and spicy. It was apparent that they were a proud, welcoming and generous, close-knit family who are always willing to share whatever they could afford.

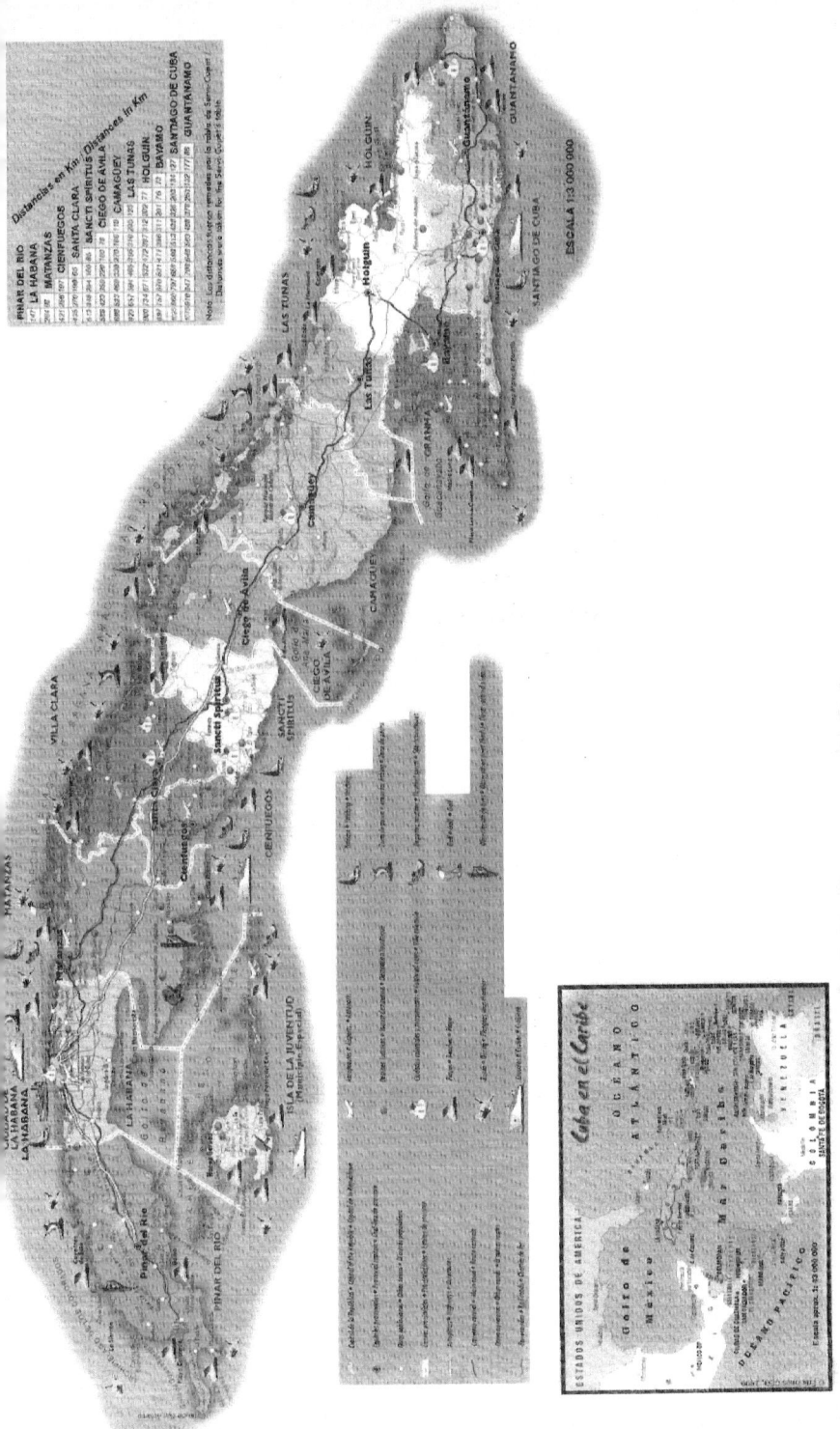

Spanish Colonial buildings in Old Havana

1950s American cars

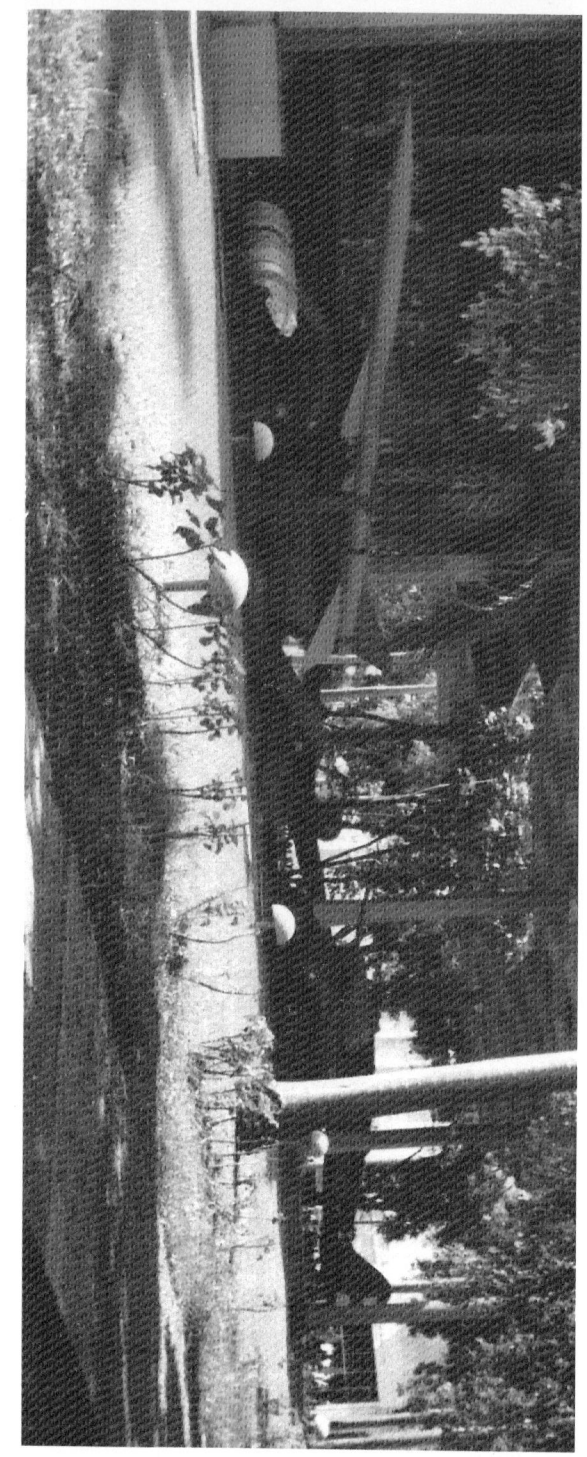

Weapons captured at the Bay of Pigs

Tank and bus used in the battle at Bay of Pigs

Havana arms museum

Portrait of Che Guevara

Cuban women in traditional dress

Plaque dedicated to Jose Marti

Havana from the air

Chapter 22

Matanzas Province

Saturday, 20th July 2002

One of the largest provinces in Cuba, Matanzas lies a hundred kilometers east of the Capital Havana. It is noted for many important areas such as Guama with its crocodile farm, Playa Larga, Bay of Pigs and the Zapata National Park, famous for its wetlands and protected wildlife.

It is a major industrial city comprising of an oil refinery, rum, sugar and chemical factories. The large bay is ideal for the shipping industry, which is vital for the island's economy.

The city has the only honeymoon hotel in Cuba. All newly-weds are given a week all-inclusive accommodation free of charge, all expenses paid for by the State.

Chapter 23

Cárdenas

Saturday, 20th July 2002

Cárdenas, in the province of Matanzas, is a peaceful and quiet town, but full of character. It is rather unusual because the main modes of transport are horse-drawn carriages and bicycles. It is a town rich in history, monuments and tradition. Generally known as the "Flag City" since the first Cuban revolutionary flag against the Spanish occupation was raised here in 1850. Situated in the town are huge monuments depicting the crab and the bicycle.

Similar to most Cuban towns, the central square, Parque Colón, named after Christopher Columbus (Cristóbal Colón), is the main location for entertainment and siesta.

Cárdenas can be described as a sugar town with the landscape engulfed by thousands of acres of cane fields. Across the skies, there are drifts of smoke plumes bellowing from the sugar refineries. Cárdenas also has the largest citrus plantation of oranges, lemons and grapefruit in Cuba.

Tomás Biart Andux, an employee at Beaches hotel, had invited me to his home to meet his family.

The house, a single story building in excellent condition, is situated on the edge of the town. It is set back away from the street, which allows for a large front area mainly covered in lawn. The well decorated and furnished accommodation gave it a comfortable and homely atmosphere.

Tomás has a fairly large family consisting of his wife, her three sisters and two brothers. I was rather amazed to learn that they all (except for the two school-age brothers) worked at Beaches hotel.

It was obvious that they were a very generous, proud and humble family who lived together in harmony.

Sunday, 21st July 2002

Most of the day was spent making preparations for my reluctant departure the next day (Monday).

I wished that I could have stayed forever. A sense of guilt was evident, as if I were deserting the many people whom I'd befriended during my visit - people who had accepted me as part of their family.

At times, I wondered if and when we would see each other again. I felt in a turmoil repeatedly asking myself questions, hoping to find answers that didn't exist.

I needed some mementos in remembrance of my trips to Cuba, so I made my final visit to Plaza America shopping precinct for some last minute gifts and souvenirs.

The rest of the evening was spent with friends enjoying the remaining hours of our holiday and discussing the events of the past two weeks.

I said my last farewell to all with much gratitude and optimism, hoping that sometime in the future we would have a reunion.

Chapter 24

The Last Day

Monday, 22nd July 2002

I started the day in a rather sombre mood, knowing that it was the end of a very adventurous, inspiring and unforgettable holiday. The two-and-a-half hour journey to Havana Airport gave me the time to reflect on my experience that seemed to last forever. For the final time, I was able to admire the clear blue tropical skies, rolling hills, lush vegetation, animals grazing gracefully, and people strolling about without a care in the world.

My thoughts concentrated on Cuba, an island that is rich in history, culture and heritage, yet relatively poor economically, but it is overwhelmingly proud to provide all educational, medical and dental facilities free of charge to all its people, where truancy, homeless children and racial discrimination are non-existent. Cuba is an island of spectacular scenery, fabulous beaches and exceptionally charming people who always greet each other with the warmest of embraces. It is a nation of happy-go-lucky people whose wealth lies within themselves and not in material possessions.

For a while I felt so sad, lonely and abandoned, but consoled myself knowing that I was fortunate to have achieved my goal that would last for a very long time.

The bustle and noise at the airport brought me back to reality with a strange feeling, knowing that my outlook to life had been tremendously transformed.

CUBA REVISITED

My Story

Part 3

Introduction

Cuba is an island of great contrast with an unparalleled history, scores of museums and art galleries filled with priceless treasures, yet there is still an acute shortage of many basic food and household items which are reflected in many of the partially empty shops. So great is the contrast, the majority of the population live well below the poverty line, not knowing from one day to the next what the next meal will be; where a tour guide earns more than a schoolteacher, and a dollar, a pen, a pencil, or a bar of soap received from tourists means a lot and is greatly appreciated. Still, I felt the urge to embark on a third visit to admire the grandeur of the towns and cities with their magnificent colonial architectures. Also, to observe the diverse landscapes, lush vegetation, palm trees swaying to and fro in the tropical breeze, the clear blue waters of the Atlantic Ocean and Caribbean sea, and the breathtaking pure white sandy beaches. This was achieved in June 2003, when my two-week stay gave me the opportunity to explore the areas of Santiago of Cuba, Pinar del Rio, Playa Larga and Holguin. I needed to get as much information as possible regarding any economical improvements that the government had put in place that might have improved the everyday living conditions of the people. The chance came when I was invited to revisit the homes and families of some of the many people whom I had befriended during my previous visits. From my observation, it was evident that there was little improvement in the economical struggles felt by the vast majority of the population. However, there were very strong feelings of determination and optimism, not necessarily for themselves, but for future generations.

Chapter 25

London Gatwick/Havana Airports

Saturday, 28th June 2003

My arrival at London Gatwick Airport (South Terminal) was another chapter in my life to satisfy my fascination and curiosity about Cuba, one of the most unique cultural and historical places that I had ever visited.

For my third trip in two years, my carrier was to be Cubana Airlines flight CU401 operated by Novair. Although check-in was rather slow and frustrating due to the large number of passengers, I was anxiously looking forward to being in Cuba.

Once again my chosen hotel was Beaches Varadero, renown for its extra friendly staff, excellent services and varied facilities.

After a nine-and-a-half hour flight, I arrived at Holguin Airport, a schedule en route to Havana. On the approach, the green fields, buildings and traffic below brought back such fond memories, I felt as if I had been away and had now returned home. It was an overwhelming feeling of belonging.

At the airport, it was intriguing to see the word "Socialismo" in large bold letters displayed on a billboard, a poignant reminder of the revolution.

My arrival at Havana Airport, in the late afternoon tropical sunshine, was one of total emotion and serenity. Shortly, I was on my way to the hotel to enjoy another two weeks of beautiful beaches, delicious food, exotic cocktails and visits to some of the most interesting locations that are unique to Cuba.

Sunday, 29th June to Thursday, 10th July 2003

My stay in Cuba gave me the opportunity to visit some of the many cultural and historical sites and buildings that are part of the island's heritage.

Once again, my trip took me to the capital, Havana, a city that is forever overflowing with life, vibrancy, charm and magic.

I was pleasantly surprised to see the large numbers of new magnificent ultra-modern hotels and business premises that had been built during the last couple of years, mainly in the affluent uptown area of the Miramar district. This was a positive sign of Cuba's successful joint ventures with other countries.

A visit to the Christopher Columbus cemetery in the Vedado district of the city, said to be the third most beautiful and famous cemetery in the world, is quite educational and inspiring.

Travelling east took me to Santiago de Cuba, capital of the orient. It is a typical Cuban colonial city, artistic, rich in history, culture and heritage with a combination of charm and beauty.

Further west to Pinar del Ri´o is the westernmost province in Cuba. It is the heart of the tobacco plantations, an area of outstanding natural beauty with its lush vegetation and rugged mountains.

Trips to other places of significant interest included: Playa Larga and the Zapata peninsula famous for the preservation of endangered species of animals, birds and plants.

Visits to Ca´rdenas for Nancy's husband's birthday party, lunch with Odalys at Santa Martha, and Emily at Varadero gave me the opportunity to meet members of their families and experience the true characteristics and lifestyles of the Cuban family.

Chapter 26

Santiago de Cuba

Situated in the east of the island, with a population of nearly five hundred thousand inhabitants, Santiago de Cuba is the second largest city in Cuba. It is a city with an abundance of history, from the birthplace of Fidel Castro to the armed attack on the Moncada Military Garrison.

Here on Sunday, 26th July 1953, a group of one hundred and sixty men and women led by Castro attacked the Moncada Army Garrison in an attempt to overthrow the dictator Fulgencio Batista, who seized power in March 1952. The assault was unsuccessful, resulting in many of the revolutionaries being killed, while others were captured, tortured and murdered. Among those sent to prison on the Isle of Pines was Castro, from where he prepared his historic courtroom defence speech "History Will Absolve Me". On 16th October 1953 he was found guilty and sentenced to fifteen years in prison. In 1955 he and other prisoners were given amnesty and released due to the massive public campaigns.

Castro then went to Mexico where he met Che Guevara and formed a revolutionary army, later to be known as the Rebel Army. Along with his brother Raul, Che, Camilo Cienfuegos, Juan Almeida and eighty-one other comrades they sailed on the yacht Granma back to Cuba to continue the revolutionary war. On 2nd December 1956, they landed in the Orient province near to the Sierra Maestra mountains and continued the war which led to victory and that took Castro to power on 1st January 1959.

The centre of the city is Parque Ce´spedes, designed on the Spanish colonial era, where people of all ages sit on benches in the well-designed gardens chatting and passing the time away at all hours of the day. It is said that sometime during the day, every inhabitant will pass through the parque. With the constant stream of huge 1950s American cars cruising around the large square, it seems that the city never sleeps.

Santiago is proud to be the "childbirth of the revolution", where the bullet holes on the walls of the Moncada Barracks are still visible with part of the building used as a museum to commemorate 26th July 1953.

With its enormous buildings, including the Nuestra Senora de la Asuncio´n cathedral and the museum – Museo Emilio Barcadi´ – with an Egyptian mummy on display, Santiago is the typical Cuban colonial city.

My trip took me to the new part of the city through the district of Sueno, an affluent area with its grid-like streets streamed with coral trees, beautiful villas and the huge circular steeled structures of the Santiago hotel.

The Plaza de la Revolucio´n is dedicated to Antonio Maceo, an unforgettable hero of the second war of independence of 1895. Here there is a statue of him on his horse surrounded by machetes, which symbolises defiance and nationalism.

The district of Vista Alegre with its grand houses, splendid gardens and sprawling trees, display grandeur of prosperity with a French culture.

Santiago has some of the finest hotels in Cuba that contribute to the large number of tourists that visit the city each year.

Chapter 27

Pinar del Ri´o

My journey took me from Havana along some of the finest scenery in Cuba, to the province of Pinar del Ri´o, 110 miles west of the capital. The province is unique for its chain of mountains, Las Lomas, the Sierra de los O´rganos and the Sierra del Rosario. In common with most Cuban towns, Pinar del Ri´o consists of some fine monuments, sprawling colonial mansions and modern apartment complexes.

This westernmost province is the heartland of the tobacco industry. The atmospheric conditions (humidity, temperature and sunshine) make the region ideal for the production of the best tobacco plants in the world.

My trip north through thousands of acres of tobacco plantations took me to Valle de Vinales, a region lined with lush dark green vegetation. The vast landscape is covered with hundreds of farms and palm-leaved thatched, triangular-shaped, huts used as curing sheds for the tobacco to keep in the humidity and freshness of the leaves. In order to obtain the best results, the tobacco is planted in stages from September to December, and is ready to be harvested between two and four months later, when the plants can reach over 4ft in height. The leaves are sorted individually, and depending on their quality, used to form different layers of each cigar. It can be said that the Cubans are the most skilled cigar rollers in the world, an art that is sometimes passed from one generation to the next.

The region's magnificent scenery can only be described as unique and magical. The valleys are lined with very rare limestone formations known as Mogotes by the local population.

The village of Vinales is relatively small, but has its fair share of Cuban architecture. Its only main street consists of many houses with sun-drenched verandas. In the tropical heat the residents pass the time away in rocking chairs.

All along the twisting roads, there are women selling mangos and guarapo, a delicious tasting drink made from sugar cane.

Chapter 28

Playa Larga

Playa Larga is a mainly residential area, which was heavily bombed by the Americans during their unsuccessful invasion of 17th-19th April 1961. The area was chosen by the Americans due to the limited access by road and the swampy land around the Zapata peninsula wildlife and national park. Although there were many Cuban casualties, the Americans' losses were far greater and within seventy-two hours they were defeated.

As a mark of respect, many monuments have been erected along the road in tribute to the Cubans who have lost their lives.

On display in Havana, by the Arms museum, there are some of the captured weapons and the tank used to defeat the invaders.

Chapter 29

Holguin

Situated seven hundred and thirty-five kilometers east of Havana towards the Oriente, is the province of Holguin, founded by Garcia Holguin in the 1520s and named after himself. In common with many Cuban towns, the main forms of transport are horse-drawn carriages, bicycles and cycle taxis. The rocking chair is a prominent feature in the doorways of houses, where the locals relax and watch the world go by in timeless motion. A reminder of the Revolution can be seen all over the town, displayed in words such as "Holguineros, al Combate!" and "Batallando Siempre". The province is famous for its contribution during the wars of independence. Calixto Garcia, a local hero of both wars, has been honoured with a square named after him, and a museum, the Casa Natal de Calixto Garcia in the house where he was born. Similar to most Cuban towns, Holguin has its fair share of history displayed in the Museo de Historia Provincial. The main square is surrounded by colonial facades on bars, restaurants and shops. In the evenings, the squares come alive with music, dancing, chatter and laughter.

The blue-green waters along Holguin's forty-one northern beautiful beaches are ideal for swimming and other water sports. The coastlines of Don Lino, Guardalavaca and Playa Esmeralda consist of historical sites, stunning landscapes of rolling hills, lush green vegetation, architecture and natural sites of interests. It can be said that the province has the most magnificent waterfalls in Cuba. With its international airport, Holguin has become a major tourist destination.

Chapter 30

My Final Day in Cuba

Friday, 11th July 2003

Once again, as I began my journey to Havana Airport, I felt as though I had abandoned the many people whom I had befriended during my stay in Cuba. People who showed me so much love, gratitude, generosity and appreciation, who took the time and effort to show me around their beautiful island, divulged their culture, history and heritage. These people were friends who gladly invited me into their homes to meet their families and share their meals. Any preconceptions that I might have had towards such loving, loyal and fascinating people were soon dispelled. Repeatedly I asked myself "why do I have to leave?" "Why can't I stay forever?" These were questions that seemed to have no answers. I felt confused and regretful as if I had done something awfully wrong. At the same time, I considered myself privileged to have met and participated in the lifestyles of a nation blessed with immense charm, inspiration, optimism, passion and talent, whose goals are clearly defined, and would be achieved no matter what or how long it took to accomplish. I tried my utmost to concentrate on the wonderful times I had had, the many historic sites and buildings that I was fortunate to have visited. It was an accomplishment that had eluded me for many decades. This had been an unforgettable experience that surpassed all my expectations and imaginations, something that I would treasure for a very long time.

In a dream-like state, I arrived at the airport reminiscing about the special affinity that I had with Cuba, while contemplating the possibility of another visit to such an alluring, colourful, exciting and hypnotic island.

CUBA REVISITED

My Story

Part 4

Introduction

During my previous visits to Cuba I had developed such passion and fascination towards the Island and people that once again I decided on another trip in June 2004.

I was fortunate to have done some extensive tours of the country in the past, but with so much more to see and enjoy it took little or no persuasion to finalise my decision.

I was eagerly looking forward to being in association with some of the most charming and friendly people that I have ever met during my worldwide travels; the many Cubans who had become personal friends and contributed invaluably towards my research.

It was hard to imagine that my visit would have eventually resulted in Beatriz Marcote Ruano (known locally as Marcote) being invited to come and spend three weeks with me in November.

Chapter 31

The Airports: London Gatwick/Havana

Saturday 12th June 2004

I arrived at London Gatwick Airport on route to Cuba, my fourth visit in as many years. Unlike my previous trips I was fortunate to have avoided the long queues at check-in due to the fact that I had arrived long before the desk was opened for business.

This gave me the advantage of being the third passenger to check-in and ample time to browse around the airport shops.

As a coincidence it turned out that the charming Cuban lady and her daughter whom I had helped with their luggage at check-in were seated next to me on the plane. We had various discussions relating to Cuba and their stay in England, which made the flight more enjoyable and relaxing.

Descending in the mid-afternoon tropical sunshine to land at Holguin Airport before the final touchdown at Havana brought back many happy memories of my previous stay on the island.

Admiring the green fields, houses and traffic below it seemed as if I hadn't left the country twelve months previously.

I was intrigued as ever to see the words "O Muerte" added to "Socialismo" to read "Socialismo O Muerte" in extra large letters displayed at the airport, the usual reminder of the revolution.

After ten hours aboard the Airbus A330-200 we finally landed at Havana Airport. To my surprise the procedures at immigration and Customs took less time than I had previously experienced.

In a ferocious thunderstorm I set off on the two-and-a-half hour drive to Beaches Hotel, Varadero. A journey that can only be described as hell raising, one I did not wish to have experienced again in a lifetime. My arrival at the hotel at 01.30 a.m. on Sunday was one of great relief.

Chapter 32

My Fourth Visit

Sunday 13th to Friday 25th June 2004

It was an unusual sensation waking up on the fifth floor of the hotel listening to the sound of birds singing in the lush landscaped gardens covered in exotic tropical plants and flowers displaying an array of breath taking multi-coloured blooms.

The early morning sunshine, clear blue skies, palm trees swaying to and fro in the gentle breeze gave an aura of total serenity. My thoughts reflected to 2001 when I first saw such scenery.

The usual warm and friendly reception awaited me when I met the hotel staff.

My stroll around Plaza America Shopping Centre was more pleasant than I had anticipated. It was hard to imagine that the staff in the bank, supermarket and at the stalls all had recollections of my previous visits. It can be said that Cubans have a natural talent in remembering faces.

I had hoped that the next twelve days would be spent doing as little as possible except to relax on the sun-kissed beaches, enjoy the delicious meals and excellent cocktails which are unique to Cuba.

However, this was soon to be short lived due to the invitations that I had received from some of the staff such as Emily, Nancy and Tatiana to visit their homes and meet their families.

This was one of my many visits to Emily, and as always the family atmosphere was one of homeliness and relaxation, which made me feel at home.

It was quite absorbing to have been involved in some meaningful discussions on various topics with three generations of the family regarding the country's educational, economical and health issues that are vital to the prosperity of the population.

A warm and rapturous reception awaited me when I visited Nancy for the third time in as many years. She and her husband Richard Morales had prepared a sumptuous meal of fish, rice with black beans (morosy cristianos) and salad. A truly enjoyable meal washed down with Crystal, a strong locally brewed beer.

Richard, a brilliant tenor and soprano saxophone player, is employed in his professional capability at Sandals Hotel, Varadero. As a present I was given a sample of his work, a twelve-track instrumental computer disc aptly titled "Sandals Sunset Time" a masterpiece compilation.

I was rather pleased to have accepted Tatiana's invitation to her home, which is situated in the residential area of Varadero; a modest typical Cuban house with the electric fan and rocking chair on the verandah taking centre stage.

Although a qualified university trained veterinary surgeon, she worked as a barmaid at Beaches Hotel since the prospect of any employment in her field is non-existent; a rather unfortunate situation, which is quite common.

Due to the extremely low salary which is set by the Government, there are many university trained Cubans who have left their professions to work in the tourist industry in order to earn a better salary.

During my discussions with Tatiana I could sense the disappointment and resentment that she felt towards the system and was rather pessimistic about her professional future.

Once again my schedule for relaxation was disrupted when I decided to re-visit the cities of Havana, Santa Clara and Trinidad de Cuba.

Havana is a city that is intensely beautiful, fascinating, inspiring and romantic. The sounds of Boleros, Sons, Salsas, Mambos and Cha-Cha-Chas can be heard blaring from every street, doorway, rooftop, window, park and square.

Twenty-four hours a day the Malecon (promenade along the sea front) is thronged with locals dancing, drinking or just relaxing. With the bustling of people, motorists hooting their horns at each other and the over-crowded camel buses, the city is always on the move.

With some 900 colonial buildings of national interest in La Habana (Old Havana) being painstakingly restored I could foresee these magnificent structures in their former glory.

My sightseeing tour took me back to New Havana, an area of outstanding beauty with its sprawling mansions surrounded by landscaped gardens, tree-lined streets and newly built huge five star hotels. It was astonishing to see the improvements that had been made in the area in such a relatively short period of time.

Another day was spent in Santa Clara, which is situated in the centre of the agricultural belt. The town immortalizes Che Guevara for his heroic actions against Batistas' army in December 1958, which led to the defeat of the dictator.

The town is proud of the part it played during the revolution and memories of the combatants can be seen everywhere.

Trinidad de Cuba, which lies on the coast of the Caribbean Sea, is one of the quaintest cities in Cuba, with its fair share of Spanish colonial grandeur.

Its cobble-stoned streets are adorned with wooden mansions of terracotta-tiled roofs, dozens of museums containing priceless works of art and beautiful antique furniture.

Although the pace of activities is much slower than the capital Havana, the city is graced with scores of fine bars and restaurants providing a wide variety of drinks and meals to satisfy the appetite.

In common with Havana the pulsating rhythm of music can be heard thundering from every location.

At the resort I found myself in the company of some very entertaining and fun-loving guests mainly from Canada, England, Italy and Latin America. A truly "down-to-earth" bunch of people they were, especially a group of six Peruvian girls who were always the heart and soul of the party.

In our group was a Londoner who remained at the poolside bar drinking non-stop for twelve hours. We were rather concerned about him since he had not been seen for the next twenty-four hours. I later discovered that he had spent the time in his room sleeping off the effects of the drinks.Throughout my stay at the hotel I always made the time to see Laura who worked in the concierge office. Along with Emily they were in charge of the concierge suites, which were located on the fourth and fifth floors.

Laura is an intelligent and stunning looking girl of Cuban and Russian parentage. Having gained a university diploma in English Literature and having been a high school teacher of a time, unfortunately due to the unfavourable conditions together with the low salary, she was forced to abandon her profession. I found her company quite refreshing and relaxing which contributed to us having some meaningful discussions in a wide range of subjects.

As the time for my departure from Cuba drew nearer I decided to take advantage of what the nightlife in Varadero had to offer in terms of entertainment. With a total of nearly a hundred bars, discos and nightclubs there was a wide choice of venues.

As to be expected there was a wide selection of drinks, and no limit to the amount that one could consume. In many of the venues the ten-dollar entrance fee included all drinks for the night. It was understandable why some of the guests couldn't stand the sight of breakfast the following morning.

Although I was looking forward to being home, the final hours of my stay were quite emotional, having to say goodbye to the many people whom I had befriended during my journey.

Once again as I made my way to Havana Airport for the Cuban flight home I reflected on the year 2001 when I made my first trip to Cuba and tried to comprehend the reasons for such compulsion that led to my fourth consecutive visit.

After some deliberation I came to the conclusion that it had to be the exceptionally easy-going people, magnificent beaches, lush green vegetation, delicious cuisines, exotic cocktails and the accomplishment of a dream that I had for over four decades.

Chapter 33

The Cubans

My nine-week stay in Cuba has given me invaluable access to the lifestyles and characteristics of the Cuban people, an experience that surpassed my imagination and expectation.

Cubans are blessed with incredible personal charisma, fascinating charm, a naturally happy disposition, and record and heart-breaking good looks, which are the envy of the world. They ooze elegance, beauty, finesse and stimulation. They possess incredible will power, determination, drive and self-motivation to build their country's economy without the interference of outside forces. Moreover, they are always striving for success in all aspects of their lives. Cubans are proud and passionate of their island, always referring to it as "our country". They are a nation who will stop at nothing until their ultimate goal is achieved no matter what obstacles are encountered along the way.

Never before have I met such a loyal, dedicated, ambitious and honest race of people. They are renowned for their broad and happy smile. It is said that if Cubans aren't smiling, it is because they have got a cigar in their mouth.

They are a sharing and happy-go-lucky race of people, always willing to share whatever they've got, which at times is the bare minimum. The Cubans are talented, inspiring, committed, welcoming and appreciative.

Cubans are always willing to invite strangers into their homes. The welcome is always warm and friendly which allows the guest to feel at ease and at home.

After centuries of foreign imperialist rule, and the imperialist American embargo since the victorious revolution, the Cubans are more optimistic, hard working, loyal, positive and dedicated than ever before. Their dedication is so great that they often move house to be nearer to their workplace.

Cubans, unlike many others, maintain a very close-knit and extended family status. In many cases, there can be three or four generations living in the same house. Children may get married and become independent, but they always maintain a close-knit family unit, like living near to their parents and always keeping in communication with each other. A sense of responsibility from parents to children and children to parents is something that can be easily recognised.

As a tradition, when a Cuban girl reaches 15 years old, it marks an important and significant time in her life. She dresses up in the most glamorous flowing outfit as if she is getting married, with her friends dressed as bridesmaids. A huge party is then held to celebrate the occasion.

Girls tend to get married at a fairly young age. With their parents' consent some wives are 16 years old. It is not uncommon to see a girl who is divorced at the age of 24. As a tradition, when a girl gets married she never takes her husband's name, but keeps her maiden name instead. All Cuban nationals have two surnames, a combination of the parents' names.

Due to the acute shortage of many basic items, nothing is wasted. Improvisation is the general norm. Evidence of this can be seen in many cases such as the way the Cubans modify bicycles to carry three or more people, and the way they use stones instead of barbed wire to build fences.

It can be said that Cuban mechanics are gods in order to keep the 1950s American cars on the road. More often than not, the parts making up the engines can be from five different countries, otherwise they make the parts themselves. As a general rule, Cubans insist that nothing should be wasted, except a smile.

They display a great deal of patience. So much so that they are prepared to wait outside the shops with their ration books for hours just to get a couple of items. Quite often the shops are empty of the basic commodities.

Cubans thrive on music. It is fascinating to hear music in every street, in the bars and restaurants, on balconies and in the parks. At times, it can be a solo musician or a band playing up-tempo Latin American music.

They are always being reminded of their past heroes, such as Che Guevara, José Marti and José Cienfuegos whose statues and photographs are displayed all over the island. Billboards celebrating the revolution can be seen everywhere. One of the most prominent is "hasta la victoria siempre".

Cubans can be described as having witty customs and habits. They never ring doorbells. They shout the name of the person that they are visiting. Drivers toot their horns continuously. Not as a matter of road rage, but as a warning to pedestrians, cyclists and other drivers.

Chapter 34

Cuba

Cuba is more than just an island paradise. It is an island of unique culture, history and character. It is rich in national heritage of priceless antiques, sculptures and paintings. The island's national heritage belongs to the nation and will never be sold under any circumstances.

Over the past three decades, Cuba's agriculture has made rapid progress. Its main export of sugar, rum and citrus fruits have improved tremendously. The production of nickel, oil and cement has been a great asset to the island's economy. Cuba produces the best tobacco in the world, hence the unique world famous Havana cigars. Its coffee is renowned to be one of the best worldwide. The island is proud of its diverse vegetation, comprising of over six thousand native Cuban plants and has an outstanding record for its dedicated conservation projects.

The country has secured many huge and vital joint ventures with various countries, such as Italy, in restoring hundreds of old colonial buildings in Havana, a massive project costing billions of dollars. Canada also has been involved in many important projects such as hotels, tourism and oil production. The Cuban/Canadian "Cubanacan" joint venture has been a great success in building the country's economy. Other foreign investors are England, Holland, Spain, France, Mexico, Chile, Venezuela and some neighbouring Caribbean countries. In the mid 1990s, many prominent companies including Peugeot, Fiat, Mitsubishi, Mercedes Benz and Unilever, have opened subsidiaries in Cuba.

All of this has resulted in a positive confidence in the country's labour market and economical stability.

Cuba can be described as the most romantic, fascinating, irresistible and beautiful island in the Caribbean. The island stimulates the senses. Rhythms of rumba and salsa greet the ears. The smell of freshly lit Cuban cigars takes the breath away. The island's magnificent beaches, rugged tree covered mountains and lush vegetation set the eyes rolling.

Cuba has over three hundred breathtaking beaches, and warm crystal waters, which are ideal for deep-sea fishing, snorkelling and driving. It has a vast landscape of evergreen forests, thousands of acres of fruit trees and exceptionally tall palm trees, some of which are unique to the island.

In common with the countryside, Cuban cities boast beautiful, well-kept, green spaces. Cuba is rich in history with its classic Spanish architecture, grand old colonial houses and mansions, ancient cobbled streets and magnificent decorative wrought iron grilles. It possesses some of the grandest cathedrals, museums and galleries with an abundance of priceless arts and antiques. The island is also famous for its exotic cocktails and in many bars up to nineteen varieties are available.

Cuba's cultural heritage is rich and diverse which makes the island the queen of the Caribbean. One could describe Cuba as an island of serenity and ferocity, where the weather can be unpredictable. On any given day the heat is unbearable, then suddenly there is a ferocious tropical thunderstorm of enormous flashes of thunder and lightening.

The history of Cuba is one of the most dramatic and turbulent of all the Caribbean islands. It can be traced back to 1512 when the Spanish landed on the island and massacred ninety percent of the native Indians. The beginning of the slave trade in 1524 and coffee and sugar cane plantations contributed to the island becoming the wealthiest in the region. The brutal treatment of the natives and slaves alike continued until the end of the 18th Century. So brutal was the Spanish colonial rule that in 1868 landowner Carlos Manuel de Céspedes led the first war of independence. His death in battle paved the way for Antonio Maceo to take command and continue the war. In later years, José Martí (passionately known as the father of the revolution) led the second war of independence, which resulted in the death of fifty-five thousand Spanish soldiers and the American invasion of 1898. The turbulent occupation and rule continued by one dictator after another until the last revolution saw Fidel Castro take power in January 1959. Honours such as arcades, statues, streets and parks dedicated to the three forerunners of the revolutions can be found all over the island.

Since the revolution, Cuba has excelled in many fields such as science, technology, medicine, dentistry, education and agriculture. In many cases, it has surpassed many of the Latin American and Caribbean countries.

Cuba is proud of its huge network of medical facilities equipped with outstanding technology and staffed by highly skilled professionals. All medical and dental care is provided free to all Cubans. All funeral expenses are paid for by the government. The life expectancy of Cubans is much higher than most of its Latin American and Caribbean neighbours. In comparison to its Caribbean and Latin American neighbours, Cuba is proud to have the highest percentage of doctors per inhabitant. It takes special care in looking after women's health, especially during pregnancy.

The state prides itself in providing institutions for day care, care services, boarding schools and homes for the elderly.

Education is provided free across the whole spectrum and is compulsory up to the ninth grade. There is no truancy in Cuba. Every child must attend school. All pupils from elementary to high school wear uniforms, which are always well ironed and smart. Cuba's education system is so advanced that each year it attracts thousands of foreign students to its colleges and universities. Cuba made tremendous progress to eradicate illiteracy within four years (1959-1962) of the revolution, prior to which over sixty percent of the population were illiterate. It is now down to zero percent. It has also embarked on an English learning programme where every employee in the tourist sector attends colleges, schools and other institutions to learn to speak and understand the English language.

In comparison to many Latin American and Caribbean countries, Cuba is relatively poor, but prides itself knowing that it has no street kids. There are no homeless kids in Cuba.

Cuba is a truly cosmopolitan island with a mixture of people of French, English, African, Hispanic, Russian, Chinese and Spanish decent all mingled together. Racism is a criminal offence, punishable by a prison sentence; therefore, it is non-existent.

Cuba insists on equal rights where men and women are guaranteed the same rights in political, cultural, economical and social programmes in the development of the country.

Although Cuba has a vast modern road network system, public transport is lacking, which makes hitchhiking a natural part of life. Cubans often spend hours on the roads trying to get a lift to their destination.

Since 1991, due to the transportation crisis, the Ministry of Transport employs specialist traffic inspectors known as Amarilles (Yellow Jackets) who help to provide transport for commuters. The inspectors' main targets are government-owned vehicles, which are easily identified by their blue license plates which as a rule should not be travelling without passengers.

I was amazed at the number of lone beautiful girls waving at motorists in order to get lifts. Unlike other countries, hitchhiking in Cuba is totally safe; therefore, the thought of being molested has never been considered. The type of transport is irrelevant. It could be anything from a tractor to a truck. The only thing that matters is to get from one place to the next.

With nine international airports, flying visits to neighbouring Caribbean islands and Latin American countries for a day are quite commonplace.

There is no other country quite like Cuba. It is the most unique of the Caribbean islands with some of the best beaches in the region.

It produces the world's most sort after cigars, a selection of fine rums, the rhythm of salsa music, combined with a unique history of Spanish colonialism and post war revolution enhance the magic of the island.

It is the destination where, as well as the guaranteed sunshine and magnificent beaches, one can enjoy the extraordinary rich and well-preserved natural surroundings.

The Cuban people are blessed with a frank, open and friendly nature, and are perfect masters in the language of hospitality.

The island has an impressive cultural and historical tradition, inherited from the African, Chinese, French and Spanish.

Cuba is renowned for its cocktails and unusual cuisines, a result of the mixture of different cultures.

Due to the peace and tranquillity that engulf the island, the all year round sunshine, wonderful climate, crystal-clear waters with its outstanding marinas and superb water sports facilities, one can guarantee an enjoyable stay to the full.

From the vibrant cities of Havana, Trinidad de Cuba and Santiago de Cuba to the natural landscaped beauty of the West, rich in tobacco and coffee plantations, Cuba offers the ideal variation for the visitor.

Over the past decade and a half, mainly due to the collapse of the Soviet Union, the economical situation of the country has changed dramatically, not by choice but for the survival of the population.

The Government needed all the hard currency that it could accumulate, which led to foreign investments, privately owned cars operating as taxis, and the setting up of Paladars (private homes being used as restaurants). The meals are well chosen, appetizing and very reasonably priced since these premises are not owned by the state.

Although tax is paid on the income there is a limit on the number of customers at any one time. These enterprises including tourism, unheard of before the early 1990s, provide much needed revenue for the Government.

In Cuba a high percentage of the country's elderly live with their children or other relatives who may spend all day away from home, working or attending educational institutes.

To address any loneliness and isolation, the Government has created rehabilitation and recreation day care centres known as Casas del Abuelo (Grandparent's Houses).

Every municipality in the country has at least one such centre, which provides socially relevant support for the thousands of senior citizens who use the facility.

The island's national program for the elderly was formed in 1978 to guarantee a dignified standard of life for this social group.

Chapter 35

Conclusion

Due to the trade embargo that the Americans imposed on Cuba, it was forced to rely on the Soviet Union for over eighty percent of its trade. The collapse of the Soviet Union had a devastating effect on the island's economy and the population. In such a dire situation, Fidel Castro masterminded an ingenious device to attract badly needed foreign currency into the island by opening up Cuba as a tourist destination. Over the past decade the island has become one of the top holiday destinations in the Caribbean.

Its magnificent beaches, turquoise waters, lush vegetation, stunning scenery, stylish hotels and villas, vibrant atmosphere and exceptionally friendly people makes it an ideal tourist paradise.

My nine-week stay in Cuba can be described as one of the best moments of my life. I was very proud and humble to have spent such memorable times with some of the most charming and adoring people in the world. I counted myself very fortunate to have shared part of their custom, lifestyle and heritage.

From my experiences, I was able to distinguish between the facts and the fictions that were portrayed of Cuba and its people. Their charm and hospitality left nothing to be desired.